# Quicksilver of the Heart

*poems of the one work*

Brenda Peddigrew

iUniverse, Inc.
New York   Bloomington

iUniverse books may be ordered through booksellers or by contacting:

iUniverse
1663 Liberty Drive
Bloomington, IN 47403
www.iuniverse.com
1-800-Authors (1-800-288-4677)

ISBN: 978-1-4502-4658-3 (sc)
ISBN: 978-1-4502-4659-0 (ebook)

Printed in the United States of America

iUniverse rev. date: 08/10/2010

Also by Brenda Peddigrew:

When the Bones find Their Singing Place: poems

SoulWinds: poems of transformation

Original Fire: the Hidden Heart of Religious Women

*To all my teachers who keep on appearing
every day —
and to the Algonquin Highlands Writing Circle
without whom these poems might not
have appeared at all...*

"The lamps are different, but the Light is the same."
(Rumi)

Awake, my dear
Be kind to your sleeping heart
Take it out into the vast fields of Light
And let it breathe…(Hafiz)

You are the light of the world…
Let your light shine before people
(Matthew 5:14-16)

We meditate on the radiance of the Divine Light.
May that Divine Light lead us
to the realization of truth.
(Dom Bede Griffiths, OSB)

The Lord of Love shines in the heart of all,
Seeing him in all creatures, the wise
Forget themselves in the service of all.
The Word is their joy, the Lord is their rest;
Such as they are lovers of the Lord.
(Rumi)

# Table of Contents

# Author's Preface

Like many of the poems in this book, the title *Quicksilver of the Heart* arose out of a very ordinary encounter in a very ordinary event. I was removing an old thermometer from the side of a tree where it had served well for a few years, when it slipped out of my hand and the glass part of the thermometer hit a large stone just at the foot of the tree. Mercury spilled out and over and around. In my rushed and futile attempts to gather it up, a thought began to grow: isn't this like my own heart? Haven't I been doing this work of gathering up the fragments of my heart for most of my adult life, and with the same results? Might it be time to try another way, like surrender? This decision changed my life.

The poems in this collection continue the journey begun in *When the Bones Find Their Singing Place* and continued in *SoulWinds: poems of transformation*. The poems in *Quicksilver of the Heart* move visibly deeper into spiritual questioning and the presence of the Divine. They have taken me into wells of grief and planes of light. They illumine the natural world and have given me glimpses into the sacredness of every single living thing without exception.

But what is "the one work" and why are these "poems of the one work?" In a recent winter, while shoveling snow, that necessary beautiful engagement with the world, I realized that work "outside" and work "inside" are really the same. When I listen to my heart and my soul and take their guidance seriously, I am really working in the outer world as well, for the quality of my presence changes then and my influence for good increases. As I get older I can see this more directly, more concretely, and the poem "The One Work" says it best. Being and doing are married, and one without the other loses transformative effect.

Finally, I am often asked how it is I write poems. There is no set time. There is no plan, or any carefully thought-out intent. There is no sweating over particular words or agonizing over length or form. The closest I can come to describing my writing process for poetry is that – like William Blake - I "take dictation." Most of the poems were written during the half-hour silent writing time of the bi-weekly Saturday morning meeting of the Algonquin Highlands Writers' Resonance Circle. Sitting silently, I open inside and wait for a word or phrase; when one comes I write it down and the rest follows, often with one or two poems being written in that half hour. Similarly, when I'm doing other things anywhere, a word or phrase will arise inside and I will endeavor to write it down as soon as I can. These "inner words" have a particular luminous quality which I have learned to respect over years.

May the poems of *Quicksilver* bless, guide and protect you.

*Brenda Peddigrew*
*Algonquin Highlands, ON, Canada*
*June 2010*

## Closing Windows Against the Rain

I used to think that God
was present only when I did
sacred things: sitting in silence
on a cushion, or in a pew, for example;
praying in a Church or saying beads;
chanting or meditating –

all of which are good,, are important.
They can settle your life, but they can also disturb it,
And often should.
They are not the end of the story.
Nor even the point. At all.

The point, life is beginning to teach me,
(now, after sixty years) is this:
God is the whole world,
the whole
world.

God is the interruption of small-sighted plans.
God is the welcoming of unexpected visitors,
the lightning storm that removes immediate
convenience,
the phone call with news of a friend's cancer
or a simple need to talk.

God is the pounding rain or the bear's approach,
the springing forth of flowers and the end of summer.
God is winter.

This moment, the moment I am in now,
whatever it holds, however calm or chaotic,
this moment opens the only possibility
of face-to-face encounter
with God –
not the past or the future –
but the hairline crack in the glass of inattention.
God peeks out: a cat's meow, a child's giggle,
a morning glory opening just that second
in a constellation of sun, earth and water.

So small is God, and so large:
the night sky, moving planets
and exploding stars:
darkness is God and light.

And I, standing in this opening of time
step through the needle's eye
as smoothly as any camel,
step through the narrow gate
into the wildest and deepest of worlds –
all while
washing dishes, cleaning a litterbox,
and closing windows against the rain.

## *Alone With the Well*

There is a dark well.
Its stones are moss-covered and damp,
barely distinguishable from the woods around it.
The well is covered by a green stone,
long undisturbed, slippery.

But I can move it, just.
I can slide it aside to look in.
The musty waft strikes me first.
The darkness, thickening
as my eyes descend, seeking
bottom, which they cannot see.

There is no bottom.
I look up and around, hungry for light,
but twilight surrounds me,
dark edges creeping closer.
I am alone with the well.

Alone with the well.
I stare into its depths.
The longer I stare, the more
I see faces, rising and falling,
people lost to me
opportunities never seen-
missed. They pull me
down with them
into the well
and

I taste salt. The well
is made of my own unshed tears.

In this well is the only water
that will slake my thirst.

## *Just Under the Edge*

Yesterday, after hours of tracking,
a seven-foot cougar was found
sleeping in the sheltered overhang
of an abandoned house
two miles from our own,
deer and dog carcasses strewn
carelessly
around his innocent lair.
Stunned before he could attack,
he was driven miles and miles from
his home to save his life.

Today I spend quality time
with two tall horses
glowing with strength and grace
threatening break-out,
licking my small hand
and carefully
gumming my fingers
eyes announcing mystery of worlds
I will never understand.

Just under the edge
of these encounters
is that trembling lake of fear
roiling the gut. Who are we
least powerful of all creatures
in the natural world?
Were it not for our guns and machines
our weapons and metallic protectors
who would we be, we who
control and direct and destroy
whatever we want to, in this world?

Even in kindness
we know not what we do.

And here are the horses
approaching with careful nudging,
nosing pockets
in playful, purposeful search.
And there is the cougar
waking today in territory not his own.

How much there is still to learn
about the world
tracking
just under the edge.

## *Snow Light*

When snow finally covered everything –
quickly it came, this year –
I breathed relief
and set out to know why.

Why – when snow means shoveling
and slippery roads? Why –
when roofs are known to collapse
from too much of it? Why –
when layers of clothes triple
just to step outside?

Still, relief is what my belly breathed.

At night I go outside
to relieve the dog Kai, and notice
a reluctance to return inside.
Night walks become longer,
even leisurely.
I am looking up at stars
and white-laden trees,
breath slowing
movement ceasing.

Snow has a light of its own.

Even when sky is too cloudy for stars
even when clouds sit on its edges
even when diminished by rain or ice
snow light glows with the radiance
of phosphorescent fish, or fairy flash.

Snow light, that unobtrusive presence
almost unnoticed except in silent gazing
gives its own light in the darkest time of the year.

So does Christmas and its ancestor Solstice.
raggedy with hype and hoopla,
conflict and sadness, pressure and hurry –
the world being too much with us
(as Wordsworth noted two centuries ago)
Christmas makes it easy to miss the light
even as – succumbing to needs for warmth –
we miss the glow of snow light.

Christmas, like snow light,
sustains a glow.
Beneath the surface frenzy
is the recurring hope of love,
the necessary longing
for the ones we love
have loved,
will love.

Snow Light
murmurs
the sweet glow of love.

## The Large Lap of Life

Seeing the mother
hold that large child,
her arms hardly able
to reach around him – or her-
(I couldn't tell)
I stopped and wondered
what had just happened
in the pit of my stomach.

I felt a turn
a shift like a bottom giving way
and why?

The child was crying
the crying
that is rageful, screaming,
twisting around in the Mother's arms,
trying to get away, to lie down,
kicking and working into tantrum,
protesting the unfair circumstances of life
the frustration of desire
the Mother's denial of this or that.

I know what this child means.
And I, edging into late adulthood,
seeing the passing of possibility –
things I thought I'd do someday,
places I'd wanted to go –
know now the limit of younger expectation.

The child is screaming
on my behalf, an eldering woman
too conditioned to good behavior
to scream and twist and kick and bite.

But the impulse is there
and so I am entranced by this large child
in the Mother's arms
struggling for something
even the child might not know.

Like myself
coming to the end
of things I can hardly name,
still a child
held in the large lap of life
struggling to twist away from what holds me
and to hold with tender patience
this smothering grief
raging against everything
I am no longer able to do.

# *The Past*

It has been said
by trustworthy
spiritual teachers
that if you want to know
how far you've progressed
on a spiritual path

go to a family gathering.

If you go home at – say –
forty-five, or sixty-two
it won't be long before you notice
that – as you leave –
you are an infant again.

So what is this seduction of old patterns
pulling at my ankles?
What sucks me in
glamoring itself
with memories and longing
until pain peaks in a contracted heart?

The past is a party game
awarding prizes that dissolve in the rain
on the way home.

The past is a doorway
to a dilapidated house.
staged and frilled for quick sale.

The past is a recipe
for heartbreak, so that – ah –
heart cracks open.

## The Long Requirement

During the past twenty-four hours
I have seen two spiders.
This is big news.
After a winter of relentless snow
and thaw, rain and ice,
even a spider –
signaling that insects
are stirring into spring –
excites my blood.

You may laugh
at this desperate noticing.
If so, you have not truly encountered
the cold threat of this winter.
the long requirement of engagement
necessary for survival,
the willingness to get up
every morning without fail,
to make fire, to bring warmth,
to step out, day after white day,
into the winter world.

Some do this inside their own souls
without having to clear snow from their doors
or watch weather for travel.
It is no different.
Winter comes to the spirit as well as to the land
and all signs of spring
even a crawling spider
are as welcome
as a July sunrise.

# A Turning

Just a little shift – that's all it was –
and the world opened. I had not thought
it so easy, nor so difficult.

One moment I could tell you
a long story of dark and doom,
of impatience, exclusive arrogance,
small seeing, my self the centre.
The next moment, with a loosening
not unlike the shudder of a snake shedding
her beautiful, patterned skin –
it all fell away, blindness removed
like some healing miracle
you don't want to see on television.

I cannot explain this turning.
I only feel its effect.

It takes, I am told,
about a week
for a python to complete her shedding.
During that time she is blind –
a white milky substance covering her eyes
until the old skin is completely gone.
Only then do her eyes clear.

Perhaps this is the way
with humans also,
blind for years and years while changes
nudge their slow way through
the dance of light and dark,
torment and ecstasy, this and that,
wearing us down and down
into the cave of surrender.

Where, finally, just at the moment
when all is surely lost
the skin of illusion pushes away at last.
Sight returns, clearer than it ever was.
And in the twinkling of an eye
the world is changed, not ended
and a turning, like heavy summer rain,
leaves the fresh world sharply visible
and keenly new.

## The One Work

The dance of snow and shovel –
this winter repeated too many times to count –
falls into a rhythm
lasting long enough
to still the mind and plunge
me
into movement of blood
and bone and their fleshy container
wrapped in layers of cloth and leather.

Breath in. Breath out.
Slide under, lift, throw.
And there it is – the frozen powder
flying through air
framed in vertical lines of bare trees
wrapped like a gift in pink and gold
morning light.

Now isn't this the same cycle
as any inner landscape?
A fall of deep snow, unexpected,
frozen, still, more than I thought.
I'm buried by the weight of it.
I close my eyes, not wanting
the work of it. Which can't last
for –
how else is motion possible
than to get out the old shovel
nicked and rickety from long use?
A lifetime of use.

My own inner compost
needs more turning as the years pass
and sometimes it's buried in snow
so deep that I keep my eyes averted
until its demand rises to a height
impossible – no, dangerous – to ignore.

Then, not unlike this morning,
I give all I am to it,
to the shoveling and turning,
to the rhythm of slide, lift, throw,
to the breath of my small being,
as long as Earth holds me upright.

Breathe, slide, lift, throw –
inside, outside –
isn't it all the one work?
And the clearing that appears –
no greater reward
inside or out.

# Enlightenment

I used to think that I was needed
but all I was doing was cutting myself
on my own sharp edges.

Rushing from place to place, person to person,
cause to cause, group to group
I didn't stop long enough
to plant myself into the firm ground
that would nourish – not just my roots –
but by bloodstream, my nerve endings
and the heart of my brain. So –
parts of myself withered without my noticing
until this cold spring day of wind and emergence.

Shadow fights for its own darkness
fearing being seen
for its surprisingly small truth.
And it's no small effort
to pull it, blind and bleeding,
towards the light, its only healer.
So many will never do it at all.
And that's a loss to the world.

But here I am, in a loud spring forest,
with nothing, nothing of any consequence
to keep me from the urgent task
of digging and diving
into the warm breathing humus
of this one particular momentary life
and all life.

Everything else, for now,
is of no consequence
if the world is to be saved.

# Lilac Tree

When that first hard bud emerged
on the lilac tree next to the back door
I almost wondered where it came from.
The icy winter, long and hard and lasting, lasting,
Seemed to seal the ground and decimate
any opening for the slightest shoot.
But there it was, facing me
at eye level, inescapable.
Clinging as it seemed to be,
winter's chains were broken.

How could it not be also with me?
I thought. How could it not be
that the hardness of my own heart –
eclipsing any possibility of a soft soul –
could also send forth a bud, a shoot,
from a place I thought
long dead or didn't even know about?

Nothing ever ends.
Nothing. Ever. Ends.
Or is finished. the green is witness
and wonder, the outward sign
of life infinite and not yet imagined.
And isn't that sacrament?
The outward sign of inward grace?

Well, grace is nothing but a slight shift,
a lifting of a weight I didn't even know
was there. But relieved at its going,
oh inestimably, ecstatically relieved.

Not much different, really
from the downy new bud on this lilac tree
or the fuzzy leaf bursting out now
everywhere I look.
And I among them, one other sacrament
emerging from the frozen season.

Winter will be back, no doubt about that .
But with every exhilarating spring
life gets larger
without and within
like the reaching lilac tree standing sentinel at the back
door.

## The Watcher

Run away. The temptation
is to run away. Oh not outside –
outside I am present and attentive –
and not a lie, for I am,
but inside I am looking for a door –
not an outer door, but an inner one,
wanting to escape the tiresome repetition
of someone else's struggle
for which I become cause and target.

This is such a long story – a lifetime, really,
beginning with the first face I could see
and continuing
as if that early experience carved a road
in unfolding reality
which I then followed, a dedicated path,
and saw as the only possibility.

Until I met the watcher, the witness,
the one who opens my eyes to know
not one possibility, but many,
not one face, but a thousand,
all me, all in this moment.
and who gives me choice
who opens the door.

# *Dark Path*

I know – this is not a new path.
Countless people have walked it before me.
Many are walking it now. A few
have given words to it, words
that give me courage now.
This is the path of darkness
and no matter how or how often
I attempt to find light,
to step off this path
into a better known one,
or a path filled (as I know now)
with false light, nothing works for me
but this dark path of hidden pain
that claims me, like a lover,
like the highest authority of the heart.

Now I stand in the moment
of knowing truth's full force
I would rather avoid, if I could:
ways I want are closed to me;
ways I wouldn't choose
are the only ones open to me
and the only path open to me
is surrender to the life
unfolding before me now.

I cannot see even an inch
into this darkness. I cannot see
to take the next step.
Now I stand still, waiting –
not for light, as I'd thought
would come, would be the way.
would open in splendour
if I just surrendered, no –

it's the dark itself
that is my only light. No wonder
that every chapter of my life
could be titled "escape."
Even as a child, I now see,
this was so. Until now
I colluded with the world's false dreams:
do this and you'll be happy,
find the right clothes (size 10), the right
vocation, the right friends,
the person who understands –
but it's all false, all
beside the point
that the soul keeps on making:

this is my life. This
is my life: these trees, this house,
this place of all places in the universe,
these people, this cat.
Every moment steeped in precarious possibility
nothing staying the same, nothing
lasting, everything satisfying for a flash.

Only this is true:
the shedding and the shedding
down to bare bone, dry and lifeless,
lying on the dark path,
finished even with the illusion
of walking.

## a corridor of doors

sometimes I see
inside me
a corridor of doors
waiting to be opened

and at the end
of one corridor
is a corner turning onto
another,
and at the end of that,
another.

lately
as the years nudge me forward
with increasing acceleration
I want to know
what is behind those doors,
every one.
perhaps this is even
why I was born.

only I, only I
can turn those knobs
to the point of opening a door.
only I can decide to open one
or to leave one closed.

so far I know this:
when I allow myself to know,
when I allow myself
to shift into awareness
of whatever is within
without censoring or rejection
not only a knob is turned
but an old bolt shifts back
a door swings open
and light pours in.

### Black Leaf

already, too soon,
(it's always too soon)
black alder leaves line the edge
of the road. Next they
will be lacy with frost
some approaching morning.
The earth turns again
a fury of hurricanes
disrupting small worlds,
power unleashing destruction
beyond our ken and keening.
Even far away, we shudder.
The world grows smaller every day,
my decision to drive or not to drive
determined by a storm
a world away from mine.

The scale at which we now
know what's happening
everywhere else in the world
stretches my singular self.
Trying to plan for next week
I lose myself instead in the weather map
carried aloft in global shifts,
cultural trends, wars and disasters –
the gift and curse of news
worn like clothes day after day.

But here I am
clinging to that black leaf
at the road's edge
lamenting its passing and all the dying
heralded by its insignificant being.
Here I am, pulling myself back
from a drowning world
by a simple turning:
this leaf, this road,
this morning, silence, now.

The soul needs no clothes.
The soul is not destroyed
by weather or war
or distant disasters, nor even
by persistent refusal to hear its voice
saying without end:
"here, now, this leaf,
this road is your being, your self.
Live here. Love here.
Rejoice in everything here, now.
This is what goes on.

The soul needs no clothes
bright being that it is
seeing into the true heart
of all things, distinguishing
what is passing from what is staying
and the black leaf its messenger and mask
all at once.

# Prime of Wisdom
*(for M. on her sixtieth birthday)*

The dying of light is glorious
clothed in crimson cloaks
trimmed in gold and deep green.
Eyes can't get enough
of this glory,
air is filled with it
doubled in lakes
as calm as glass
on an October day
in Indian summer.

The dying of my light, your light
is just as glorious. Now
is our real prime,
the sum of years
a tincture of wisdom
that has been distilling itself
all these years:
every breath and vision
every ecstasy, loss and tear.

May the tincture distill further.
May it glow and concentrate.
Then
may it drop
into the ocean of light
staying you, staying me,
in continuing the mystery.

# Communitas*
### (for G and M; A and C)

Just last week
the world felt small as a clenched fist
the impending winter
a blow to the gut-
not with beauty but with tasks
and impending storms,
work piled like a threat:
snowclearing and wood-carrying,
day after day after day.
It all loomed, a tight squeeze.

Then, between breaths,
unbidden, even uninvited,
fullness unfolded,
and the world opened
like lily petals
revealing centered gold.

Light appeared
loosening the clench
and it was more wonderful
than I can tell you
except to say
that Light was present
all the time. Light
and a kind of glowing comfort
made visible in food and laughter
stories and wonder.
The world held us tenderly,
and so we held each other.

## II.

The golden leaves
carpeting the ground
are the same leaves
that three weeks ago
were the forest's wallpaper.

This laughter and these eager gifts –
books and insight, travel and new
disturbing questions
have become now
a sweet, aching silence,
time's scrapbook
holding a timeless collection
of gratitude and loss.

What is all this coming and going
except time unfolding the world –
that great barge, bowing and surging –
sometimes too slow,
sometimes too quickly,
always towards a place
we cannot sufficiently name:
***communitas.***

*"***Communitas*** is the shared experience of adventure in the face of something so worth living for as to be worth dying for, the common commitment to an impossible dream, radical and revolutionary, imaginative and indomitable, energetic and exultant, fragile, ferocious. Only ***communitas*** can seek the wind, the Spirit who will fan the flickering flame into a roaring fire…" (Gittens, 2000)

## *Sliver of Light*

It's alright to say
that I want to reach
a place of peace, a place
undisturbed by struggle
and dissension,
but the truth is –
if I would ever open my heart to it –
that the world is not
as I would like it-
it's I who must find
that sliver of light
in a lifetime of wounds
that announces
the world as it is.

And the world lives, eats, drinks,
vibrates in opposites. There really is
no light without dark,
no good without evil,
no pain without comfort.
There is no life without death.
Ah! There's the trick of it.

For most of my life
I chose only light,
only good,
comfort, life,
railing against their opposites.
Lucy-like, I wanted all ups.

Now, after years of battle,
I am smiling at my own innocence
and open the hands of my heart
to the link of light that binds the opposites
together.

That's where life is. And I –
I am dwelling there,
choosing neither one nor the other
but sleeping peacefully curled
in open hands.

## *Waiting Their Turn*

What words hide
beneath this hurried,
encrusted surface?
Hiding, but waiting too
words waiting to come out of the dark
words intensifying their meaning
in captivity, words
patient, but not infinitely so.
"One day," they say, "one day"
as they sense the light
on the other side of the wall
holding them in.

Meanwhile, the grass greens up,
the trees flush with leaves and needles shoots,
the rivers run, and lakes rise and fall.
Color flourishes and skies
desperately offer hard healing rain,
day after day.

And the words wait their turn,
gathering close to the small door,
sensing the immanent moment
of release, of outpouring,
of their bursting and delicate expression
linking one world with another.

## *All to Say*
*(Christmas, 2008)*

Christmas, yet again.

This year, the economic world
rising and falling like a thermometer,
Christmas as we know it
comes with a sharper edge
than its shallow
glittering and teeth-aching sugary aspect,
which is harder to maintain
when faced with panic and despair.
Not as much energy left
for the hype and the mindless spending
not as much incentive
when retirement funds and daily expenses
are as threatened
as the price of gas.

All to say
this might not be a bad thing –
that we take a deeper look
at this secular feast of greed
and false plenty, at this
panoply of illusive expectation.

Christmas belongs, after all,
not only to the Churches
but to the earth –
the light returning, first and foremost –
and the Light of the World
born in a stable with nothing-
hear this: nothing at all
but animals and kindness.
How did that
get to this?

But this year,
this year of chaos and agitation,
this year of desperate hopes
and fearful threats,
this year of wars and rumors of wars –

Christmas could be
something welcome
in its original simplicity
its hidden repetitive reality,
its one shining moment
of birth and welcome.

The world never stops moving
and the speed of it is hastening.
We are swept in its torrent,
caught and carried
to places we might never choose.

Yet even there, even there,
some moments sparkle
as unexpected as a Christmas tree
on an early dark evening.

All to say, all to say
I don't want to miss them.

This year, let Christmas shine with simple surprise
shorn of complaints of too much of everything.
Let balance come back into our tilting worlds
however briefly.
And let us be overcome with gratitude and Light.

All to say. All to say.

## Perfect Timing

What is it about Christmas plans
that take a shape of their own, glittering
with expectation, dripping with gaudy lights,
assuming the world will conspire
to dress that particular stage with everything
my own longing creates like a contrived photograph?

A lesson learned, invaluable, truth-dressed,
carving away self-deception like a Japanese blade,
leaving  a small flame, undressed -

By the light of that, I see that what happens
is the only thing that can happen,
that what is asked of me
is what is asked of everyone living,
and that what is asked of us all is
Presence. Being present, we walk, we breathe,
we speak, we love, we act –
shedding illusions like last month's skin.

When I planned a different Christmas this year,
Returning to my original home after a long time away
from Christmas there in all its loud and chaotic
uniqueness,
I assumed it would happen, just as I planned.

But dying and death intervened from the first moment,
catching my breath with their perfect timing.
I would not have chosen it, but it was chosen for me,
and I could rail against it or dive through a small
window
into timeless truth, which I prayed to do and mostly did.
Peace ensues.

The perfect timing of life's unfolding,
disregarding small plans and expectations
offers its blinding light, just at vision's edge.
I see it. I see it.

## Lately a New Voice

Lately a new voice is making itself heard
deep within the usual cacophony
that hardly sleeps, hardly rests,
except during those few moments
when that merciful drop
to the dark bottom of awareness
opens a new cavern of wordless, thoughtless
something. Is it presence?

Too soon for names.
But the whole world changes there,
becomes a place I do not recognize
cannot manipulate.
Control is as ineffective
as car wheels on clear ice,
careening when it tries, off base,
irrelevant.

For moments, the world of my body stills
as if blood wasn't streaming everywhere,
as if there was no heartbeat or shifting muscle,
no impulse to move,
a thousand things to be done.

The new voice sometimes sounds out words
I don't use often enough:
praise, trust, thanks, surrender.
Peace. Be.

This new voice is content with the world
and with myself in it. This new voice
carries me like a rushing stream
towards a waiting lake
and I am breathless and content with the ride.

I wait. I turn toward it as often as I can,
as often as I dare, and sometimes
I'm too frightened to sit waiting for it to arrive.
The old voices return, then,
catching me up on all I've missed and heard
a million times, spilling over me like an infant
throwing up milk on my shoulder,
reminding me of all I've left undone
and that needs, needs, doing.

## What If?

Perhaps it is that I am only now
passing over into light
with all its handmaidens and attendants:
Truth, Clarity, Peace
Accepting Things As They Are,
and eyes shorn of any lenses
but their own.

Truth alone is hard enough to bear,
takes practice as strenuous and disciplined
as any daily workout,
but being in every moment's truth
is marathon training
in this world of canonized illusion.

The oldest of all battles:
light and dark, truth and lies,
goes on as always and always will.

But what if? What if
it were all one, not either this or that?
Not pitted against each other
like eternal enemies?

Would not then the flow of life
be a river of dancing shadows
moving into an ocean of light?

# Revelation

Confusion is a friend, opening the door of welcome,
offering a moment when everything opens and
everything
is possible again. Confusion
shakes the kaleidoscope,
life's colorful pieces
falling into new patterns and new empty spaces.

Certainty gives answers
before questions arise.
choking them off before they see sun's light.
Certainty is the enemy,
guarding its gate against possibility,
against visions
rising like the moon over a dark landscape.

As Rumi said before me
"how great was my knowledge
before "Revelation made me dumb."
Questions are doorways
into wisdom without beginning or end.
Answers fall away like ash,
blown by the slightest wind.

There is more strength in taking off the armor of
certainty
than in shining its breastplate, hour after hour.

Confusion propels a new language,
and that language, knowing its limits,
falls into magnificent silence: Revelation.

# *When Sisters Gather*

*(for the Presentation Sisters' Leaders, New Orleans, 2009)*

When sisters gather, laughter arrives. Voices
young and old erupt in seeing the new world
moving beyond the possible
that was the seen path just a moment ago.

When sisters gather, stillness settles into that real
moment
of breathing together. Then breath continues
into conversations, into necessary decisions of the day,
claiming them for Larger Life.

When sisters gather, decisions emerge as if waiting
just behind a door like polite children being invited to a
party.
It was ever thus and so, and of course we can do that
when home claims us again.

When sisters gather, life looms large and light weaves
them
into a wool tapestry of warmth and rich color,
each a thread the others can't do without
if the picture is to be complete.

When sisters gather, fire sparks and flames consume
what is no longer needed. Clean visions emerge in
words
no one thought to speak before, words
that were always there but unlit with recognition.

When sisters gather, music wraps them round like a gift
given to everyone they know. Notes dangle in the air
sung in silence as loudly as in sound.
Sisters sing, and send their singing out like their own
souls.

Sisters gather.
Love exchanges itself.
Being is in communion.

# First Snowdrop

The whirl-a-gig
of things needing attention
never ends.
Futility of effort
spins and twirls
gaining momentum
until momentum
carries on alone
and stopping requires
wrenching force in itself.

Yet here I see
shadows of trees
moving inch by inch
over March snow.
Here I see the slow melt
edges shrinking daily
until sudden disappearance.
Here I see intercourse
of sun and wet earth
birthing, birthing
a snowdrop there
that wasn't there yesterday.

If I allow this ground
this air, this river
to teach me
my looking alone will
slow me, slow me
slow me
to earth's pace
to steady unfolding.
Without push, without resistance
without drama or encouragement
I listen for the voice
that tells the snowdrop "now"
and I will stand up
and flower.

## Everything Else in Shadow

Two white bars of light, slanted
parallel on the scuffed wooden floor:
everything else in shadow.

Doors that were once wide open
swung back, inviting and warm
now as closed as stone
not a crack of opening, not an inch of give,
knocking and pounding
to no avail.

Who is that person in a lifetime of pictures?
The thinnest ribbon of connection
is there, but that's all. Another closed door.
Or the books that almost jumped open,
off their shelves, into my hands –
now as closed as padlocked doors.

Inside me once was a room
joyously crowded with the furniture
of expectations, anticipation,
comfortable assumptions –
that room, that room has been cleared out,
is now
a silent emptiness dusted with relief.
On its old wooden floor
shine two white parallel bars of light,
slanted, parallel,
everything else in shadow.

### Feet Against the Sky
#### (in shoulder stand)

Standing on my shoulders outside
one blazing spring day
I suddenly saw
my feet against the sky.

Well, first I saw the sky
the blinding blue of it,
and then my feet,
big toes perfectly parallel
serenely still, like a painting.

I gazed for a long time
while blood rushed to my head
and the whole of my body
settled into candle-quiet.

Sometimes everything in the world
changes places with the sky.
This spring, all I see
are winter-felled trees, brutally shorn,
still unfolding delicate leaves
as if nothing happened,
as if they're still standing straight.

And the goose whose early nest of eggs
was swept away when the river flooded,
now serenely nesting again,
though her mate is doubly protective
this second time.

Just this week,
Trout-Lily and Dutchman's Breeches
sprouted where the worst of late ice
lingered longer than usual,
and red trillium, eight in all,
bloomed overnight
where none had been last year.

I realize that my own feet against the sky
started something, shifted
how I see the world.
A window opened, and opened
inside as well as outside. I see
differently, now that assumed foundations
have turned upside down
when I wasn't looking
and just when I thought
everything was safe

I saw my feet against the sky
and the whole world changed.

## *Inhabiting the Real World*
### *(seven questions)*

In the real world,
faces wrinkle and hair turns gray;
early or late: does it matter?

In the real world
older is wiser, younger still learning.
One inward, the other outward; aren't both needed?

In the real world
things are necessary, stuff is luxury;
where is the line between?

In the real world,
food and water enough for all, earth included:
How many choices are too many?

In the real world,
children are future, elderly, treasure:
how does caring take hold?

In the real world
people are more that the eye perceives,
luminous with spirit, eternal and whole:
where is the window into this vision?

In the real world,
time is illusion, everything is now –
where is the threshold?

Only through a narrow gate
do we inhabit
the real world.

# *Star-Flower*

Wandering without purpose
I found this one
star-shaped flower,
tiny as a dime
suspended, mid-air.
half-hidden
in the tumult of new green
that is sudden spring
after a brutal winter.

Where have you been? I asked.
And how have you survived
that long blast, that frosty blanket?
Here needle-thin stem swayed
and my eyes
couldn't seem to get enough
of her delicate design
laced among her star-arms;
in fact, I removed my glasses
to get a closer look.

Then my breath –
strong enough to make her sway
became a bridge, she dancing,
me filled with a delight
outside all Time.

Like a queen, she bowed
and like a servant, I bowed back.

I have no doubt now,
that she saw me,
and that the air of attention
I'd breathed her way
opened the cosmos,
micro, miniscule,
and in it,
I knew my place:

no more, no less
important than her own-
the star-shaped flower
tiny as a dime.

## Contradictions

This morning. this
early spring, struggling green morning,
birth and death, cold and warmth
jostling for presence, hope
and despair, rising and falling
like the stock markets –

this morning I see the contradictions
that hold the world together.

When Blake etched Job
lying on his back, overcome
with helplessness and rage,
he placed the image of God, author
of all trials and troubles,
parallel to Job's body,
hovering a foot above him,
bearing down, oppressing. If you look
along God's body to the left,
you see with shock
that God has one cloven hoof.

What are we to make of this?
Except that God
is the author of all, all
that we call terrible
as well as good.

If this is so, then the nature
of God, the nature of life itself
is contradiction, is flowing change,
is coming to be and passing away –
all from one source, not two.

And if God is Love, then
where does that leave us
who cannot be good, cannot
shatter our positive thinking,
our plaster-saint illusions?

We know now that a hot-enough fire
transforms disparate materials
into something new
and previously unknown in the world.
Perhaps the same holds true
for spirits, for souls.

Meanwhile the delicate trees,
tender in shoot and bud
continue the cycle which leads
to death, and on the way
flow and flow through change after change,
not contradictions,
but transformations.

## Wind's Imperative

Many things I used to think important
are now falling away.
I can hardly begin to name them
but I'll try a partial list:

Dashing around "getting things done."
Crossing items off a list.
Going to meeting after meeting,
after meeting.
Contacting people
who don't return the favor.
Buying clothes for recreation.
Talking on the phone.
Checking emails too many times a day.

Something is slowing me down, calling me
in another direction, simple and present.
Something is sounding: a deep chime, whispering
go outside,  be with animals,
turn within, listen to the wind,
hear your own voice, stop now!
Trees speak and soothe.

Pages these imperatives would fill
but it doesn't fill me yet. I can't
get enough of this endless being
this unfolding, surprising, river of life
the wind at my back,
nudging, pushing, turning me
without my prior knowledge.

Between one breath and the next
Life opens and closes
like a tree shaken and stilled
while it stands rooted
in the hard good earth.
Wind decides everything.

## *Flaming Wick*

If I can take a step
If I can relinquish my tight hold
on things-as-they-should-be,

If I can let go of that lust for certainty
and leap into what-I don't-yet-know
and trust the Light said to be there,

If I can remove the lid from
from that jar of moldering rot
that occupies some corner shelf
in a seldom-visited inner cellar,

Then every day might just become
a surrendered prayer to Light
and I a flaming wick.

### *after sixty*
*(for A.L)*

after sixty the world
opens its shell
and you glimpse
a pearl you had always suspected
was there, even sought,
but here it is now,
winking at you
from inside
its stretched-open
carapace.

# Tracking Light

A small white flame seared one branch
in the black forest. Walking along the road
my eyes were pulled to it, fiercely,
as if a wild and threatening animal
had appeared.

But it was only the sun,
that most familiar of all stars,
tip-toeing through the damp density
to illumine that one branch
so brightly that my eyes stung,
seeing every needle standing in praise.

All my life, I've been tracking light,
seeing its smallest spark
in the darkest of places.
All my life, light
has offered itself to me
like quicksilver, appearing
and disappearing, keeping me still
and releasing me to roam.

I don't know how it is
I will leave the world
but I do know it will be more
birth than death
when the time comes, because
all my life I've been tracking light.

## What the River Asks

The river smells, this early spring night,
like birthing waters and new blood,
like rain before it falls. Presence,
not judgment, is what the river asks.

The river holds spiral and flow,
death, fertility, abundance. It holds
a way to be fully in the world..

# And So the Day Begins

I love getting up on a morning
when the day feels empty, spacious,
filled with the emptiness of the possible..
I yawn and stretch, not rushing
out of bed. I fantasize about
what I'll write  that day and how quiet it will be.

And so the day begins
but that's not the end of the story.

The phone starts. I check email and
six need answers today.
The cat bawls and bawls to go out, only (as I know so
well)
to do the same operatic performance
about coming in sooner than you'd think.
The fire needs another log. The dog needs a walk.
Someone in my family is in crisis.
Oh, my students are due another assignment.
The pipes spring a leak.

And so the day unfolds.

It used to be that I'd lose ground here. I'd fall into
chaos,
irritation and annoyance being words too small
for what I'd be feeling. The day
seemed owned by someone else and what a cruel trick
my waking thoughts (and the whole world) had played.
I turned into a frantic, lost and shouting siren.

And then one time, when I was least expecting it,
the day brought me a gift.
A small window opened and I saw – I saw
the still point inside me pulsing light
and everything else swirling around it,
the light steady and untouched.

It wasn't that the day changed –
it still goes on with its unpredictable urgencies –
but I have less attachment to them now.
I know another place and so the day, my teacher,
opens windows and sometimes doors
and I step through into the primary claim of light.

## *Shift*

With quiet sigh
I turn away
No further hope of comfort there
The dark and deep alone
give stillness name
but wait -
the Great Bear of Love
is dancing still, and merrily.
Growing up is imminent!

## Inside Everyone

There is a word
waiting to be spoken
inside everyone who lives and breathes
in the known and the unknown world..

The word is made,
not of letters, but of light.

Sometimes the word is stuck
behind a locked door
with rusted hinges.

Sometimes it lies chained
beneath rotting floorboards, pulsing,
or kept in the attic
with no possibility of escape.

Sometimes the word
hums a puzzling tune
in its prison,
patiently living a prisoner's life,
waiting for release.

Often the word attempts to escape,
leaking out suddenly,
surprising the one who speaks it,
the one who stuffs it back into the dark
as quickly as possible.

For the word is made,
not of letters, but of light.

And when the locked doors are opened,
when the floorboards are pulled up
and the attic hatch pulled down;
when the word needs no escape
and is spoken, shouted, and announced
from rooftops and high hills –

then Light blazes and blooms,
dark corners revealed and released.
And the word made not of letters
but of light,
illumines the world.

## *Chroi Baile: Home for the Heart*

Autumn is a gathering time
not only of harvests
but of hearts.


Summer scatters.
In this world of virtual relationships
and easy travel; in this world
of hype and high speed and the increasing momentum
of days colored with lists and demand after demand,
summer opens doors and throws us out
like children whose mothers
want a bit of peace at whatever cost.
Summer stirs the pot
and we whirl in a hundred directions
sometimes at once.


then the first leaf turns color
and catches our evasive eyes,
seducing us with colors often seen
and just as often forgotten. Red
burns into skin; yellow calls for sunglasses,
bronze evokes awe. Breathing mist and
a sudden azure sky jolt us into awakening:
stop here.


The countryside and the small towns
empty of visitors settle back
with an ambivalent sigh of relief.

Now we come together again.
Now we seek out the steady companions
of winter. Now we begin again the deep work
of holding hidden threads of connection,
of community, of ready neighboring of one another
with the unpredictable guests of winter.

Autumn is a gathering time
not only of harvests, but of hearts.

Chroi Baile: the heart's home:
fireplace of communion,
magnetic compass of warm certainty
and potluck dinners
layering life in harvests of hearts.

# The Great Unfolding
### (for G.)

No more looking back now,
except from a solid shore
observing a distant island over calm waters.
No more beating bushes already beaten
too many times
or finding my feet stuck
in sinking holes of mud and ice –

We've come to open groves, you and I,
green spaces to stroll and be silent
wrapped in warming gold
light beyond what we ourselves
could create or even evoke.

What brought us here?
What unforeseen opening in a dark sky?
A fine fiery stream of anger,
an opening window in a longing heart,
and willing arms that reached out
believing the ones already reaching back.

Thus it is that Light breaks open
a closed hard world, such sudden surprise
that former forts and stony defenses
melt away like beams of light
dancing and bowing in the Great Unfolding Dance
of being alive, the dance of no ending.

## Grace

Grace is a wild card, a
get-out-of-jail-free card,
and the cards fall around us like rain
at every moment,
as close as breathing.

When the world shifts, turmoiled weather
outside and in, I – being the world –
shift with it. Cells rearrange themselves.
New understandings download in my shaking system
like surprising software.

This is a time of initiation.
This is a time of release, of protecting perceptions
now shooting like fireworks into a black sky.
This is how seasons change:
one day a soft summer breeze
the next a cold wind ripping tender leaves
from their branches.
One day, a snow-blanket; the next
snowdrops and crocuses.

Can the soul grow any differently?
Really…I am no different than earth,
my body, my body also her
water, blood, soil and air,
her cycles disguised in my every breath.

Knowing who I am is the only thing
that separates me, yet – knowing
changes nothing as I move through
that tender screen of invisible threads,
that curtain of compassionate light
covering the world.

All I can say now is this: I tend my soul
like the garden that it is becoming –
not a walled garden, but a fruitful,
overgrown patch of soil,
bursting with forgotten seeds
and unpredictable gifts
dropped by passing birds.

Fireworks pass.

## *It Comes*

Every day we walk
in the small breathing space
between worlds. My world
and yours, our world
and theirs, this world
and the world just there
on the other side
of this thin veil.

Every day we wake and make
a blind way through time tunnels
toward the last lying down each night.
Between the dark sleeps
days unfold like an accordion,
fingers finding notes of harmony
and discord, harmony and discord.

For the first time
I feel them both as one,
as weeds and wheat
impossible to separate,
all glowing with the life
of that one spirit
lighting everything.

It comes.

# The Storm's Heart

Swaying branches of high trees
are whipped and slapped amidst
blinding drifts of  blowing snow
like riffs on a keyboard
like modern dancers on a white stage
stealing breath and certainty.

In snow wind I struggle to stand,
leaning and bracing, a dancer myself
on nature's winter stage,
plunging forward for wood, for walking,
for human necessities diminished
by brutal cold and blinding snow.

The world is more complex
than I ever imagined it to be
and I am just finding it out.
In this last third of life
the layers fold open
like a kaleidoscope. I can't
track them all. Nor do I have to-
that's the best news, that –

and the solid roots of high trees
buried now in careless icy snow,
unmoved by the wind's whip
and the snow's drift, claiming ground
by standing still in the storm's heart.

## How I Know

I don't know how I know –
my body knows-
that the earth beneath my feet, beneath the snow
is stirring her green shoots, waking them up.

I don't know how I know –
my body knows –
that sky is  lightening, sun strengthening,
while woodpeckers announce an early spring.

I don't know how I know-
my body knows –
that every tree I see is calling now, calling out
to the sap that hid in its roots so long ago.

I don't know how I know –
my body knows –
that the elements of love
shift and meld unforeseen in their golden alchemy.

It's not my eyes that tell me these things;
it's my body that knows.

## Night Sky

The night sky, with its singing stars
burns messages into my heart
in a language I have yet to learn.

The stars speak fire.
They radiate themselves
towards my expanding heart, while the moon,
that silent lit lamp of steady truth,
expects nothing except my eyes' attention.

Well, she has it –
that grandmother of all and each,
one by one. Everyone who has lived
through all of time has wondered
at her mysterious companioning,
lying on her back, surrendered,
or smiling down – down, mind you,
like a wise grandmother of unspeakable age.
Which she is.

But the night sky is a welcome blanket,
familiar as fingernails or toes or a soft pillow.
Best to greet her, warmly, every night,
lest I burst open like a seed pod
in her burning silence.

# White Woods in April

After green shoots have started sprouting
from the black damp soil,
after heat has forced the skulking away
of the last snowy patch, hiding in the shade,
after shielding eyes from the sun's strength
in stunned surprise –

one morning in April I wake to the world
all turned white again, air frosty enough
to nip bare skin, to force mitts and hat,
to plunge the soul back into winter's grip.

How like the way of things, this sudden dip
into ice after days in warm sun,
sand warm enough for bare toes,
while ice clings to the surface,
playing with waves.

How like days unfolding, coasting along
on the dip and rise of household tasks,
phone calls and firewood, work and rest,
even while the next rogue wave
readies its powerful surge,
its sudden shock of icy cold.

This morning, walking in the white April woods,
a light rose and shimmered from the spring snow
and spoke to me of the undying pattern,
the rhythm of breath in and out,
of light and dark, and of how
they are all one, inseparable,
and never opposing one another.

The white woods in April
are gone by noon,
shedding their morning costume
and returning their attention
to all that is being born in the deep leafy ground.
The shimmer remains.

# No Light

## I.

In the tight crowded birthing chamber
of black soil, shot through with sharp stones
and the feisty hold of melting winter ice,
there is no light, no light at all.

So how does that fresh green shoot
know to begin? Where does its order come from,
and who speaks it?
What magic nudges the lime green upwards –
green even in that tight, lightless ground –
defying gravity of water and earth
and blind darkness?

The first snowdrop outside my door
elicits this heart-stopping question.
The white bloom, delicate and drooping,
defies even the dirty snow still surrounding it.
Everything in nature mirrors every other reality
so the snowdrop fairly shouts
from her insignificant piney patch: "Look inside!
Look inside!" so I look
and find no light.

## II.

Begin here. Begin.
Rest your face, your tired limbs
just here, against this damp stone.
this shifting soil, wet with possibility.
Trust dark. Trust wet. Trust the shift
that will come, but not by your command
and never by your timeline.

Wait. Deep in that crowded soil
the birthing chamber is hidden, waiting.
Deep in that dark soil, everything you need is poised
awaiting that mysterious command.
Deep in that dark soil
the voices that know hum and wait, hum and wait,
standing ready
to unfurl that first green shoot
when light – how? from where? by whom?
penetrates the impenetrable.

### As Usual

The morning came -
a frosty April morning
with cold and sun negotiating for the day,
with last year's leaves awaiting earth's digestion,
and succulent daffodils
bravely facing down the frost –

the morning came, when –
standing still by the depleted spring river,
facing the early sun,
my heart's resonance
vibrated like a tuning fork
to some unknown Light.
It opened like a water lily
From its tight bud
And filled my body with a kind of trembling,
Dissolving and shucking off a hidden structure
Like the shedding of dragon scales.

Now what? I thought.
What's next? And how do I live without this
familiar, contained and predictable heart?

I am seldom where I'm standing,
mind somewhere other than body,
soul split, pulled here and there
like a disregarded dog.

But this resonance,
this trembling and dissolving and vibrating
like a great symphony of presence,
this music
stretches me into beyond what was,
and – ker-plunk, ker-plunk –
the fresh, red, steady centre of being and body
takes me, as usual,
from the only solid moment
into the next.

# Lupin Light

In the fresh light of earliest morning
I came upon lupins standing forth like a host of angels
streaming with radiance in their royal colors,
holding forth in a silent sermon
that delighted not only my eyes
but the soul of my heart.

Soon they would blacken, turning to seed
and giving back in another way –
not just in that quietly lit presence,
but in the deeper commitment of falling
and dying and releasing,
believing without doubt in next year's spring.

All these things and more
the lupins whispered to me
in their choir'd presence.
All these things and more
did they reveal like a secret
held for centuries.
Wordless, thoughtless, weightless,
I stood and received,
transforming as they were
and in the same timeless time.

## If So

I cannot get over how light
silently appears in the dark forest
early each morning,
nor how they find the two
find companionship,
peaceful and each itself
without rancor.

And why should there be rancor?
Each is what it is, illuminating its opposite
just as my own heart both soars in light
and sinks into the terrifying grief
that grounds it.

Could it be that one does not exist without the other?
Could it be that we are not meant to say one is best
but to find that peaceful place inside
where both have a home in their appropriate time?
Could Blake's etching be true – that the God
oppressing poor Job with unspeakable trials
has a cloven hoof?

If so, if so, then the world as I know it –
all those battles of beliefs and laws
that torture the innocent – isn't
the real world at all.

# *a word longing for letters*
### *(for Presentation CLT)*

In the house
where poet Hopkins sometimes summered
from the dampish dark
of Dublin buildings in winter

the ones who live there now
say – as nonchalantly as pouring tea –
"ah yes, he's here – there are those
who hear footsteps on the stairs late at night-
it's probably him."

And I, sitting in a room writing
in the night's quiet before this exchange
feel a stirring of something, a rustle,
a presence – not of steps or sounds –
but of friendliness, just there –
a word longing for letters, an eye
opening in the dark,
a slight unfolding making its slow way,
like a leaf, like a seed breaking open
before it even knows the light.

By the time I begin to comprehend
the multiple mysteries and momentary surprises
in this unfolding world, I will be too old –
or perhaps too wise - to speak what I know.
Nevertheless, I trust now
that the difference I make is seen
and in the seeing shifts the world
towards good.

## *Pillar*

At first I thought that the tears inside me
were a well, bottomless and unknowable,
but now I see they are a pillar,
filling my vertical frame and spreading
into fingertips and toes.

Looking back, I remember the pillar of salt
just in time. That pillar of salt served
as a reminder, as a sentinel of sorts,
and so does mine.

It's time to surrender to the life
I have knowingly and unknowingly
chosen. It's time to give up thinking
I know what any detail of another's life
should be, including my own.
It's time to flow outward,
pouring from that pillar of salt
like a stream of light
like a surprise redemption,
like the grace of God
I never knew myself to be.

## All Along

I carved a path inside myself
with words – other's words –
and finally, my own.
Words were salvation,
were sustenance, were connection,
were love. Words saved me
from chasms and bottomless pits
and oceans and gravity.
Words saved. Faithful guardians –
they never failed me

until one morning
when the luminous books
lost their glow
and an unexpected flame flared
like a flower at a path's end
in the place where words used to live,
My body
opened and revealed
the wordless light
that had been there, illuminating words
all along.

## *Quicksilver of the Heart*

On this longest day of the year
my heart woke at first light
writing poems, lines of words
streaming and dancing like a hidden stream,
like the aurora borealis, like rain
falling in its misty curtains.

My heart in a shimmering gown
dances its quicksilver dance
refusing to be silent, loving what it loves,
without mind's cattle prods and prisons.
My heart's quicksilver ecstasy stretches
into pulsing stars and leaps at the sight
of one Blue Flag Iris that wasn't open yesterday.

The still morning air, dripping with honey light,
witnesses as much to darkness as it does
this glowing radiance, and my heart knows this –
knows the rise and fall of temperatures, knows
how the god Mercury – or, if you like –
Hermes the messenger – never ceases
running back and forth with his winged feet
between heaven and earth. My heart follows

I would not have it any other way

I would not have perfect control –
how small my world would be then,
how insignificant in this great work
of a new world being born. Instead
I am forever dancing
with everything there is – every
change of weather, inside and out,
every small green shoot of every plant and tree,
every ant that builds its inspiring nest,
every shimmering glow and lesser star
in the dark stormy skies.

I could go on and on in a litany
of the quicksilver heart
but love knows no boundaries
and anyway is always awake,
exploring in every direction,
uncontainable as mercury
escaping a thermometer.

A quicksilver heart runs
like blood through the veins of the world
bringing love
to the darkest of places, indiscriminately
cradling rich and poor,
living and dying
stone, plant, human, animal –
all running over
with the given light of God.